Snap books

DRAWING Wild Animals

BY ABBY COLICH

ILLUSTRATED BY JASON JUTA

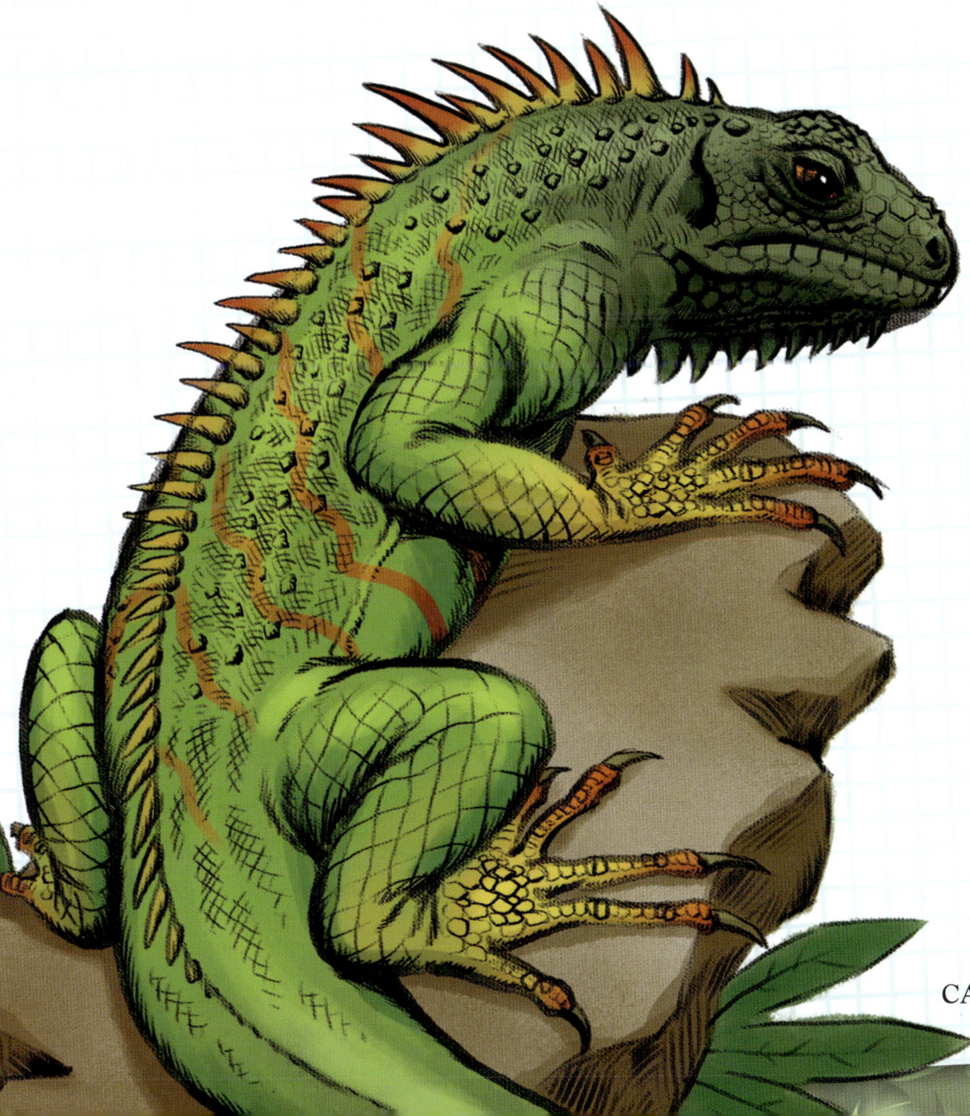

CAPSTONE PRESS

a capstone imprint

Snap books are published by Capstone Press, an imprint of Capstone
1710 Roe Crest Drive, North Mankato, Minnesota 56003
www.capstonepub.com

Library of Congress Cataloging-in-Publication Data
Colich, Abby, author.
Drawing amazing animals, drawing wild animals / Written by Abby Colich ; Illustrated by Jason Juta.
pages cm
Summary: "Gives readers easy instructions on how to draw different wild animals"—Provided by publisher.
ISBN 978-1-4914-2132-1 (library binding)
1. Animals in art—Juvenile literature. 2. Wildlife art—Juvenile literature. 3. Drawing—Technique—Juvenile literature. I. Juta, Jason, illustrator. II. Title.
NC780.C583 2015
743.6—dc23
2014033157

Editorial Credits
Juliette Peters and Charmaine Whitman, designers
Aruna Rangarajan, cover designer
Laura Manthe, production specialist

Photo Credits
Design elements by Shutterstock

Printed in the United States of America in North Mankato, Minnesota.
092014 008482CGS15

Table of Contents

Getting Started

From the graceful gazelle to the powerful polar bear, the world is full of amazing wild animals. Animals are fun to learn about and fun to draw too. Whether you're skilled at sketching or new to the world of drawing, you can have fun filling pages with a wide variety of animals.

Young Elephant

Adult elephants are the largest land animals on Earth. But young elephants have some growing to do. They don't have their white tusks yet, but they do already have large ears that help them stay cool in the heat.

Step 1

Step 2

Step 3

Step 4

Final

TIP

Once you've mastered this young elephant, draw one that's all grown up. Just make it larger and add the tusks.

16

17

Each activity includes a description of the animal, steps to show you exactly how to draw each creature, and a tip for when you want to get creative and mix things up. If your gorilla turns out looking like a glob or your ostrich is awful, don't worry. Drawing takes practice. If you mess up, it's OK to start over again. Just remember to be creative and have fun while you work.

Tools of the Trade

Drawing is a fun and inexpensive way to express yourself and your creativity. Before you get started, be sure you have the proper tools.

Paper

Any white paper will work, but a sketchbook meant just for drawing is best.

Pencils

Any pencil will do, but many artists prefer graphite pencils made especially for drawing.

Color

A good set of colored pencils will give you many options for color. You can also try using markers or paint. Many artists enjoy outlining and filling in their work with artist pens.

Sharpener

Your pencils will be getting a lot of use, so be sure you have a sturdy sharpener. A good sharpener will give your pencil a nice, sharp point.

Eraser

Be sure to get a good eraser. Choose an eraser that won't leave smudges on your clean, white paper.

Electronics

Many great apps and programs allow you to draw on screen rather than on paper. If you want to give this medium a try, have an adult help you get started. Learn all the features and functions before you begin.

Zebra

Known for its black and white stripes, this relative of the horse sticks out from other animals in the African savanna. Scientists believe zebras' stripes help them blend together in the eyes of their predators, making them more difficult to catch. Each zebra has its own unique stripe pattern.

TIP

A zebra's stripes extend onto its short-haired mane. Don't forget this detail when drawing your zebra.

Step 3

Step 4

Final

Ostrich

The largest of all birds, the ostrich can't fly. But what it lacks in flying it makes up for in super speedy running. It uses its two strong legs to run from predators. An ostrich will even kick a predator with its two-clawed toes if cornered.

TIP

This dark brown ostrich with white wings is a male. If you want to draw a female ostrich, make all the feathers a light shade of brown.

Step 3

Step 4

Green Iguana

Green iguanas love eating plants and climbing trees. These lizards are covered with soft, leathery scales. Spines cover their backs from head to tail. Don't skimp when drawing this creature's tail. It can be just as long as the rest of its body.

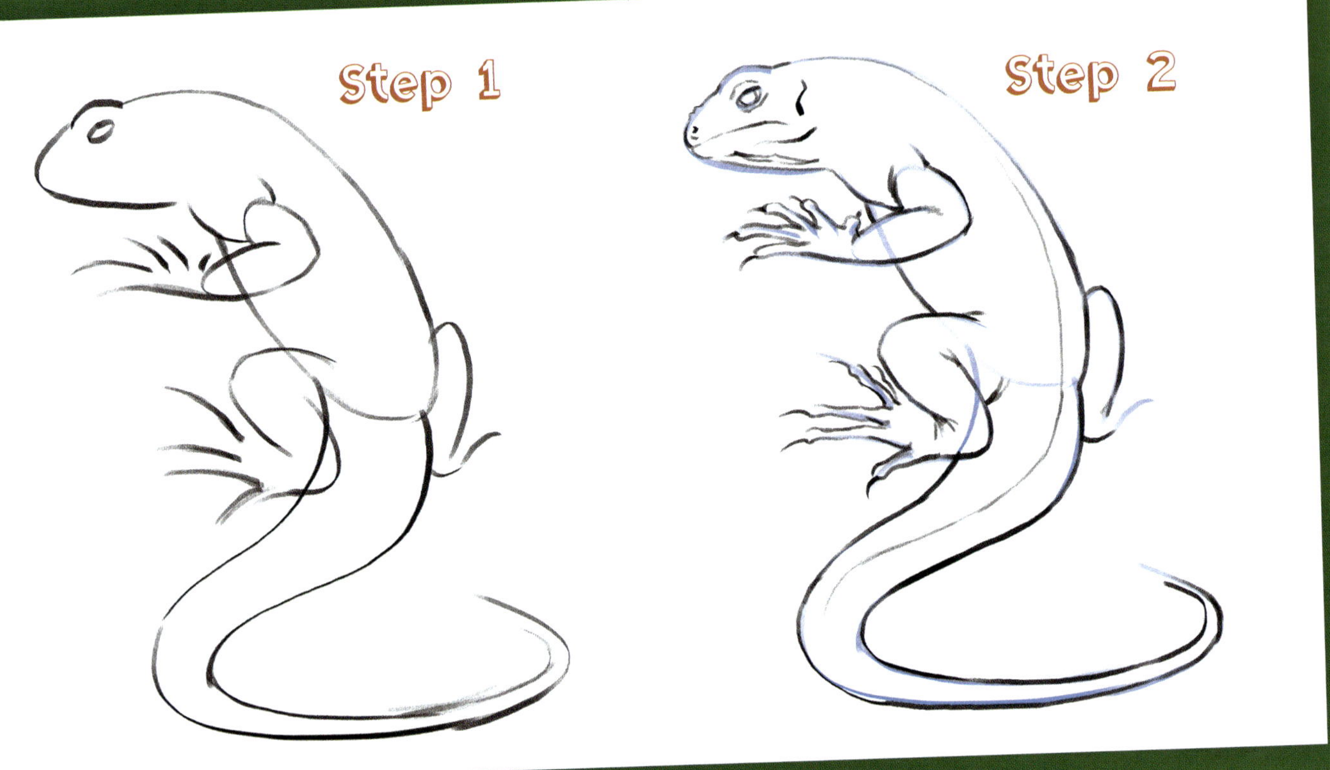

TIP

An iguana's strong tail makes it an excellent swimmer. Try drawing a green iguana in the water.

Step 3
Step 4
Final

Gazelle

The gazelle, a type of antelope, is mostly beige with a lighter underside. Some gazelles have white on their faces or darker markings on their bodies as well. In addition to being speedy runners, gazelles leap high in the air to avoid predators.

TIP

Some female gazelles don't have horns. You can draw your gazelle without them.

Step 3

Step 4

Final

Black Jaguar

Jaguars are rare in the wild, and black jaguars are even rarer. These jaguars are shiny and black all over. The biggest cat in the Americas, jaguars prowl the jungle floor hunting for food. Unlike other big cat species, they are also skilled swimmers.

Step 1

Step 2

TIP

Jaguars usually live alone unless they are raising young. Try drawing a mother jaguar with a cub.

Step 3

Step 4

Final

Young Elephant

Adult elephants are the largest land animals on Earth. But young elephants have some growing to do. They don't have their white tusks yet, but they do already have large ears that help them stay cool in the heat.

TIP

Once you've mastered this young elephant, draw one that's all grown up. Just make it larger and add the tusks.

Step 3

Step 4

Final

Gorilla

This great ape is the largest of all primates. It meanders through the rain forest walking on all fours, a movement called knuckle walking. Most gorillas are black or brownish gray. Their humanlike eyes are brown surrounded by a black ring.

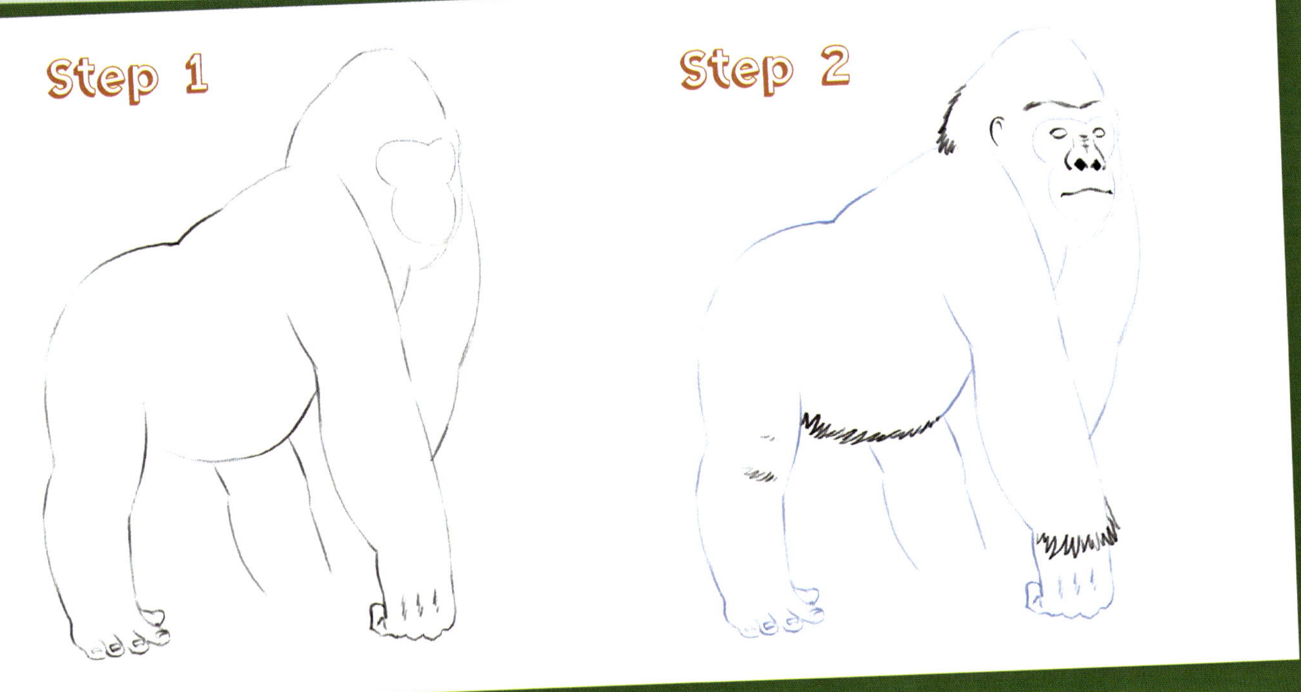

TIP

One gorilla subspecies is called the silverback. You can make your gorilla a silverback by giving its back a silver tint.

Step 3

Step 4

Final

Alligator

The alligator's body is armored in bony plates called scutes. A strong tail makes this reptile a pro at swimming in swamps and wetlands. Don't forget the nostrils on top of its long snout. These holes allow the alligator to breathe as it swims just under the surface of the water.

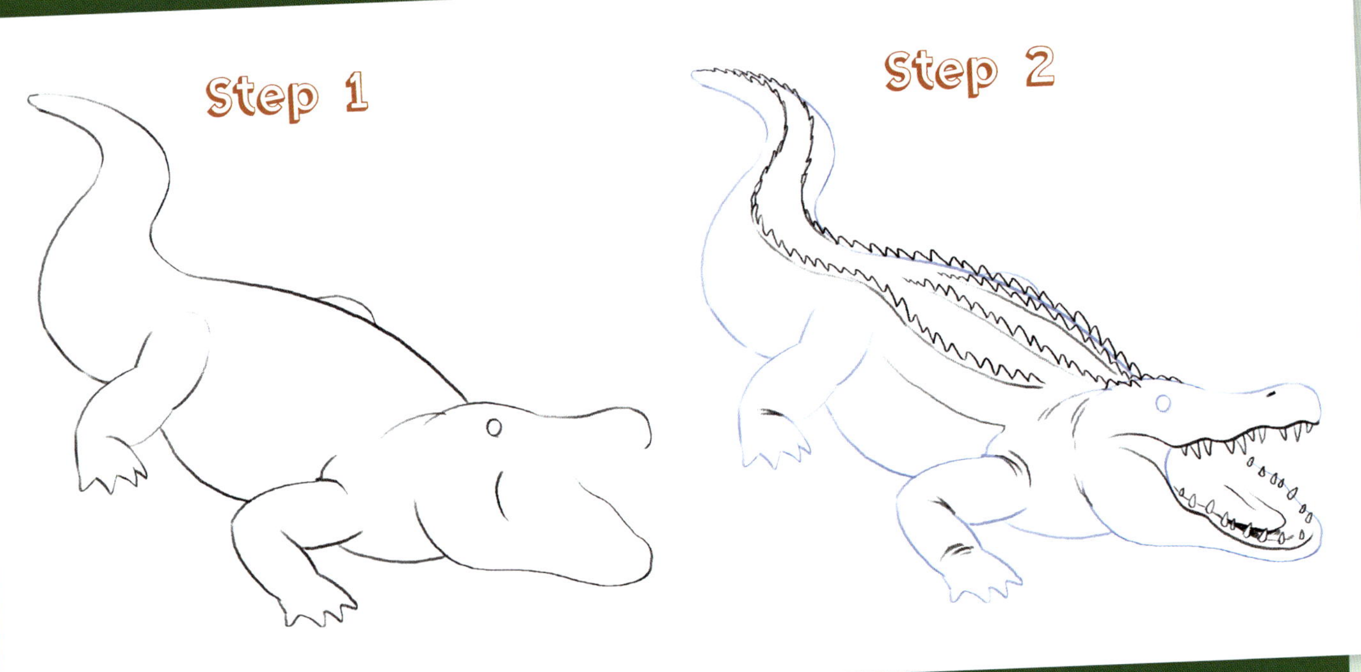

TIP

Frightened by this large creature? A younger alligator might be more your speed. Draw a smaller alligator with yellow stripes down its body.

Step 3

Step 4

Final

Giraffe

The tallest animal that lives on land, a giraffe's long neck makes it easy to recognize. This mammal's hair is a light cream or white. Its spots are orange or brown. Both males and females have a pair of hair-covered horns called ossicones.

TIP

Each giraffe's spots are unique like a human's fingerprints. Draw your giraffe a companion with different markings.

Step 3

Step 4

Lion with Cubs

Lions are the only social species of cat, living in groups called prides. They are also the only cat species in which the males look distinctly different from the females. Brown manes encircle the heads and necks of the males.

TIP

Want to draw your cubs with their mom instead of their dad? Just draw the lion's body without the mane.

continued on next page

Step 4

Step 5

Step 6

Final

Polar Bear

These hunters of the Arctic have fur all over their bodies to help them keep warm. Fur is even on the bottoms of their feet to protect their paws while walking on the cold ice. Their whitish fur helps to camouflage them in the snow.

TIP

Female polar bears usually give birth to one or two cubs at a time. Try drawing a mom with her babies in a snowy den.

continued on next page

Step 4

Step 5

Step 6

Final

Internet Sites

FactHound offers a safe, fun way to find Internet sites related to this book. All of the sites on FactHound have been researched by our staff.

Here's all you do:

Visit *www.facthound.com*

Type in this code: 9781491421321

Look for all the books in this series!